T0114850

Through it All

A Journey of Faith

Linda Thomas

authorHOUSE®

AuthorHouse™
1663 Liberty Drive
Bloomington, IN 47403
www.authorhouse.com
Phone: 833-262-8899

© 2021 Linda Thomas. All rights reserved.

No part of this book may be reproduced, stored in a retrieval system, or transmitted by any means without the written permission of the author.

Published by AuthorHouse 03/02/2021

ISBN: 978-1-6655-1516-0 (sc)
ISBN: 978-1-6655-1528-3 (e)

Print information available on the last page.

Any people depicted in stock imagery provided by Getty Images are models, and such images are being used for illustrative purposes only.
Certain stock imagery © Getty Images.

This book is printed on acid-free paper.

Because of the dynamic nature of the Internet, any web addresses or links contained in this book may have changed since publication and may no longer be valid. The views expressed in this work are solely those of the author and do not necessarily reflect the views of the publisher, and the publisher hereby disclaims any responsibility for them.

The scriptures were taken from the King James Version. Public Domain

Contents

♥ Standing with Faith ♥

Chapter 1

I WANT TO TELL you this unbelievable, horrifying story about a woman who fought and battelled three years of cancer without any surgeries. She did it all by standing with faith and believing in God's control because she knew being diagnosed with cancer was going to be a tough thing for her to accept.

It is about a woman that could not eat a healthy diet, especially during the first stages of her chemotherapy and radiation treatments. At this point, she should have been eating a more nutritious diet and on track to having a consistent diet routine.

I am talking about a loving and caring lady who is a firm believer in the Lord—trusting her Lord to help her regain an appetite. This lady is a fighter, and she tried day after day to sit up in bed without getting sick.

This woman kept encouraging herself to put food of some variation into her mouth to gain nourishment.

She soon realized the hardship in trying a simple routine task, such as eating. Drinking liquids was also becoming a challenging task to keep in her stomach. The this and that days of her illness created a burden for her. It was a challenge to swallow anything or hold any liquids down.

The more challenging days began to get worse. For instance, trying to remember things, much less keeping up with the reality of life. The long days were turning into weeks. It was challenging for her to find the will and strength to get any nutritional food that would stay on her stomach.

Her body was losing taste buds, and from that moment on, nothing appealed desirable to her.

Still, keep in mind, she was also bleeding from the rectum and having pain in her stomach. The pain would bring you to your knees, and it made her feel dreadfully sick.

She could not imagine how she would function or find the energy to get up for the day. How would she make it work and still carry on her job duties working with Alzheimer's patients?

The reason being is, well, let us go back to where it all began. I want to explain how it felt when one had been diagnosed with colon-rectal cancer.

The year of two thousand thirteen, she went to a clinic down from her neighborhood. Inside that clinic, there was a doctor on call who checked her out.

She was in a lot of pain and agony, plus there was blood in her stool. She thought to herself that it would be something simple, like hemorrhoids or something of that nature.

From that day on, she knew the painful, horrible burning sensation that she felt all the time was real. It was an unwelcome pain, and it was trespassing through her body, triggering havoc in her life. I can tell you that it was like no other person could fathom.

The doctor who saw me on call that first night at the hospital might have recognized that the problem could have been cancer. If she did, she had nothing to say about it. However, that doctor on call sent her right away to a colleague friend of hers that very same day to better diagnose her condition more clearly.

The doctor suggested a colleague with an office in the downtown area near the hospital. Her colleague was a professional GI specialist and was more experienced in the field of colon-rectal cancer, and they were able to see her at once!

When she arrived there in his office, things were moving too fast, and her mind was fearful. The pain she was suffering was unfamiliar to her. It was hard to define a pain that was an excruciatingly painful and burning sensation in her abdomen. It seemed so different from her lingering stomach pain, and it kept her wondering what the exam results would reveal.

♥ Why Me Lord ♥

Chapter 2

THE GI SPECIALIST told her that she had some sort of colon-rectal cancer. He was 99% sure but still needed a colonoscopy exam to confirm his diagnosis for insurance purposes. Once the colonoscopy results were in, she was to follow up with him to discuss the results.

She was stunned already from the news he had given to her. She cried a little, then laughed and thought to herself, not me! "I don't have cancer." While dealing with denial, there she was waiting in suspense for the results from her test. News that she could only think about and ask, "Why Lord, is this happening to me?"

Still remembering "Through It All," this lady was always a healthy eater. She knew a lot about nutrition and exercise from working as an activity associate for years. She held an 8 hour a day job, working 40 hours a week plus overtime, attending to her Alzheimer's and dementia patients' needs. She was a woman who has always been a positive, energetic, vibrant believer in her faith.

Let us stop for a moment. I want to pause right here in this chapter and explain something to you.

The woman I have been writing about in this book is myself _ _ _ _ I could not fully understand the news of what was happening to me next until the actual colonoscopy appointment took place.

When it all was said and done, the finalization of knowing the truth about what was causing my pain and suffering finally appeared real to me after learning of the final diagnosis.

I felt like something from my gut was trying to put me through a test of my faith. Then out of nowhere, I experienced a feeling of indescribable pain that put me into a different time zone.

Suddenly life was not fair, and it was essential to keep faith in God's control. I knew right then and there that his love would cover me because this was a real revelation. A sign for us to trust in His power.

Something came over me that day, and I remembered a scripture from the bible.

> Isaiah 53:5 (KJV) [5] **But he was wounded for our transgressions**, he was bruised for our iniquities: the chastisement of our peace was upon him; and **with his stripes, we are healed**.

Surprisingly, I never would have thought that it could have been me. Usually, when you see a doctor, you get a prescription that will help you feel better. It was apparent that this journey was not going to be that easy for me.

My husband was there holding my hand and comforting me while I got the news from the doctor. It did not appear real; nothing made any sense to me. Reality had me thinking of my perception of fear.

The acronym for FEAR is –

"False – Evidence – Appearing – Real"

I knew then it was time to acknowledge the truth of me having the cancer disease. As the old saying goes, "It is what it is." For example, if the sky is blue, then the sky is blue, and this was not the time to be in denial. I knew it was time to dig in and trust in God with all my heart.

To trust in his purpose and plans for my life by acknowledging the news of having full fledge colon-rectal cancer. To trust in his grace and protection to undergo the next steps to be taken with the upcoming chemotherapy and radiation treatments.

There is a scripture in - Proverbs 16:9 (KJV) [9] A man's heart deviseth his way: but the LORD directeth his steps.

♥ My Faith ♥

Chapter 3

I T MADE ME stop to think how lucky and blessed I was to have God's grace. I am grateful to my husband for taking me to be seen by the first doctor. It was knowing very well that I was reluctant to get any shocking news.

Still "Through It All," I was thinking I am a healthy, faithful, strong woman for having colon-rectal cancer with faith. I knew the aspect of my life had a purpose and a plan.

My faith in God became more vital than it ever had before. I looked over at my husband and friend, who told me sometimes we need only to pray.

Like it says in the bible verse.

Psalms 118:8 (KJV) [8] It is better to trust in the LORD than to put confidence in man.

Often, things happen to us for the glory of God to help us and others to believe. I honestly thought that I had faith until I began to deal with this cancer journey thrust upon me. Somebody told me that this terrible cancer would be hard to go through and that some will survive, and some will not survive.

I was having panic attacks and started to have all kinds of thoughts towards uncertain feelings. I thought in my head that I was living in a nightmare. A nightmare so frightening that it was hard to open my eyes long enough to acknowledge this disease.

This journey was not going to be easy, and the doctors ordered two rounds of chemotherapy and thirty-five radiation treatments.

When God has a plan, he directs us, and he orders our steps through the journey.

> Isiah 55:11(KJV) [11] So shall my word be that goeth forth out of my mouth: it shall not return unto me void, but it shall accomplish that which I please, and it shall prosper in the thing whereto I sent it.

He is using me as a vessel to write this book. Why, because it is a story that will touch people's lives and allow me an insightful way to introduce the true meaning of faith,

"Forward – All – Issues – Trusting – Him"

That means we have faith in our Lord! "Why," because we read in the scriptures –

> 2 Corinthians 5:7 (KJV) [7] (For we walk by faith, not by sight:)

He is our all-mighty God! Many people have gone through cancer and have not had the opportunity to live. That was not the way the cards I received fell on my behalf.

I was one of the many fortunate ones that have survived this cancer disease.

I had such a strong will and the desire to survive, not only for myself but for my Lord and Savior most of all. And secondly, my soul mate, who is my husband.

I am also grateful for the support of my family and friends during these treatments. I am also blessed to have met several young and old cancer victims along the way.

♥ Identity and Individuality ♥

Chapter 4

LET US PAUSE here for a moment because I want to explain my perspective of cancer.

First, it is a deadly disease that no one can understand unless they have experienced it themselves. It is impossible to explain the pain involved with the intense treatments of chemo and radiation. Or how one is to deal with the loss of appetite and the cost of losing your hair.

It is mortifying for a woman to lose their hair. A woman's hair is an essential part of her identity and individuality. Well, do you remember the old phrase "not one hair out of place?" That was me always trying to have pretty hair.

It was hard to wear crochet hats, beanies, and knit cap toboggans, in the Texas summer heat. I was blessed to receive a variety of headcovers from multiple people throughout my journey.

I know it came straight from their hearts, and I considered it a blessing and honor to wear these precious gifts.

Secondly, it is still a fearful thought that after three and a half years later that there is the possibility that cancer could come back at any given time.

Thirdly, seeing people looking like zombies after having one chemotherapy treatment after another. The worst thing to see for anyone was to sit and watch their loved ones go through these treatments. They were stuck with needles and (IVs) in their arm, while blood transfusions also took place in that room.

It would make a person want to cry for hours. Most of the time, at the chemotherapy treatments, the families would be praying for the treatments to work. Individuals were voicing powerful prayers trying to bring a semblance of peace to everyone in hearing distance.

You see, chemotherapy is most often given as an infusion into a vein (intravenously). The drugs can be provided by inserting a tube with a needle into a vein in your arm or a device in a vein in your chest. Some chemotherapy drugs can also be taken in pill or capsule form.

I know that chemotherapy was the strongest of all treatments and is a form of poison that flows into your body.

I was a 51-year-old woman in a great deal of pain, which was still alive and standing when this all came about. I remember that I was just barely making it.

There can be other reasons for pain besides chemotherapy, such as cancer itself. The pain may be related to chemotherapy, and doctors can treat it by Giving pain-relieving medications, blocking pain signals from the nerves to the brain with spinal treatments or nerve blocks.

The medications that I was taking were all-powerful, like Xanax, Hydrocodone, and OxyContin. Sometimes the pain was so severe that none of the combinations of medicines were of any help.

It is a miracle the pain medication I was on did not cause me to become an addict.

I thank God it did not kill me.

♥ The Rollercoaster Ride ♥

Chapter 5

THE TREATMENTS AND medicines made me sicker and sicker. Hours later, it started to take over my body, causing me to run to the lady's room to throw up.

Another way of explaining how it made me feel was like being on a rollercoaster. It was like a theme-park ride or the ones at the carnival. The one that forces you to stick to the wall while the floor slowly drops out from under you.

It is like you never knew when you woke up if you were drifting out into another world. Like that ride, my life was spinning out of control, and these were the difficult days of my life.

Getting out of bed became more of a challenge as I struggled day by day, trying to focus on something to eat that did not taste metallic. Even trying to get up and move around was a hassle.

The seconds turned into minutes, and the minutes turned into hours, and time was slowly slipping away. I wanted to give up, but my faith in God would not let me. Nor would my family or friends let me give up.

My health declined, and I was going down quickly, losing weight, not wanting to go even one more step. I remembered my sweet friend, whom I have known for 16 years, asking if she could get me something to eat?

I responded, "I am hungry for some lemon ice cream from Braum's," Wow! That was a good wake-up call from God. It started as a good this and that day for me.

I finally started trying to eat something!

I also remember that it was several days after that time until my husband took a spoon to my mouth to encourage me to eat again. He would not quit nagging me until I did eat. I gave it my all that day and still could not get enough strength to taste the food without feeling sick.

It especially made me feel like my world was spinning around and around, just like that carnival ride I rode on when I was a little girl. I remember my dad, mom, sister, and brothers rode it when we went to the Galveston beach for our family vacation.

I had ridden on it before. It was like a centrifugal force that made you stick to the sides of the wall with the floor moving away from the bottom, and when the ride was over, it made you want to throw up.

Let me try to explain this more clearly.

I was very dizzy, still not understanding why I had to experience this feeling of extreme nausea. I never gave up, and I found a way to believe in my faith, that God had a purpose and a plan for me.

With God's protection and the doctor's help, I knew it was going to work. It was a sign that the Holy Spirit was with me "Through It All."

♥ Peace and Quiet ♥

Chapter 6

I HAD THE LORD by my side and pointing me to scriptures from the bible. For instance, in

> **Jeremiah 29:11** (KJV) 11 For I know the thoughts that I think toward you, saith the LORD, thoughts of peace, and not of evil, to give you an expected end.

I then realized God was in control of his plans for my life and future. Here I was, a skinny, puny person and losing significant amounts of body mass. I was down in weight to only 93lbs.

I just was not in the mood for anything but sleeping, and I wanted nothing else, just peace and quiet. I mostly wanted people to leave me alone.

It was hard for me to focus on my workplace, which was always there for me "Through It All." Helping me to keep my job position as an activity associate. With their help, I was able to maintain my job duties day after day while taking chemotherapy. Then after 8 hours of work, I would go for my radiation treatments.

Let me try to describe how those 35 treatments were like for me.

It was like standing in front of a fiery blow torch from hell for 45 minutes at a time after working all day. Most sessions, I felt like I had baked in an oven with fire coming out of my rectum. I honestly thought I was walking around in a world that I have never known before.

I was thinking to myself if any of this was even real.

My husband noticed one day how I was talking like a robot. It was due to a lack of oxygen and nutrition to the brain. It was getting harder and harder to keep my mind on work or even have the energy to walk towards the kitchen and get a drink or something to eat.

Let me tell you another horrible experience that happened to me.

My Hyperbaric Chamber Dr. ordered 60 sessions of treatments. The reason for all of this was so I could get my oxygen back to a normal level. Someone mentioned that it would start making me feel a lot healthier and begin to feel stronger.

He counseled me to explain what I would be feeling like when going down in the water. He said it would be like you are scuba diving many feet down in the ocean waters, then feeling like you are going up in an airplane and being jet-lagged all day.

I honestly went "Through It All" at 6:30 am – 7:45 am every morning before my work schedule, dragging myself to start the rest of my day working.

When I started work, I went to the floor to do my job activities with the residents. There in the hallway was my dear sweet friend Ella.

As I approached her, she put her arms around me and prayed for me. Her prayer was for me to believe in God to take all control of these painful (this and that days) entirely away.

To lift me on his shoulders just like the bible tells us in,

> Deuteronomy 33:12 (KJV) [12] And of Benjamin he said, the beloved of the LORD shall dwell in safety by him; **and the Lord shall cover him all the day long, and he shall dwell between his shoulders.**

Here in the bible, it is saying the one the Lord loves shall rest between his shoulders. The bible tells us that Jesus bore many stripes for those who believe in salvation, and we shall be healed.

❤ Barely Surviving ❤

Chapter 7

Aᴸᴸ ᴏꜰ ᴛʜɪꜱ brings me back to this question. Has anyone had faith that was so powerful it could move a mountain?

> **Matthew 17:20 (NKJV)**
> **20 So Jesus said to them, "Because of your unbelief; for assuredly, I say to you, if you have faith as a mustard seed, you will say to this mountain, 'Move from here to there,' and it will move, and nothing will be impossible for you.**

That scripture came to me one day as I was attending an Alzheimer's patient of mine. She had a flash memory moment about this scripture from her past, and we enjoyed a serious conversation with one another.

Well, let me tell you that I have that kind of faith in God. I have never lost it because by believing in the grace of God, I have made it "Through It All."

I want to tell you about another big challenge I faced day after day. During the rough part of the treatments, I almost died while working at my regular job.

I went to work daily with a chemo bag strapped to me and a port in my body. I was barely surviving one rigorous treatment after another.

Working with Alzheimer's and dementia patients was not always an easy job for one to do. It was hard for me to focus on my work due to the episode of **Chemo Brain Syndrome**.

To explain what this term means, **Chemo Brain** is a part of your brain that loses cognitive thinking that has been affected by chemo treatments.

Chemo Brain is a common term used by cancer survivors to describe thinking and memory problems that can occur after cancer treatment.

Chemo Brain can also be called chemo fog, chemotherapy-related cognitive impairment, or **cognitive dysfunction**. The sometimes vague yet distressing mental changes cancer patients notice ***is real***, ***not imagined***.

They might last for a brief time, or they might go on for years. These changes can make people unable to go back to their school, work, or social activities or cause it to take a lot of mental effort to do so.

Chemo Brain affects everyday life for many people with cancer. For years people with cancer have worried about, joked about, and been frustrated by the mental cloudiness they sometimes notice before, during, and after cancer treatment.

Even though its exact cause is not known, and *__it can happen at any time when you have cancer__*, this mental fog is *commonly called* **Chemo Brain**.

Despite the many questions, it is clear that the memory problems commonly called chemo brain can be a frustrating and debilitating side effect of cancer and its treatment.

I also developed a case of **C Diff** twice.

The meaning of this C Diff, *__Clostridium difficile__*: A **bacterium** that is one of the most common causes of infection of the colon in the US. Patients taking antibiotics are at risk of becoming infected with C. difficile as antibiotics can disrupt the bowel's normal bacteria, allowing C. difficile to become established in the colon. In some people, a toxin produced by C. difficile causes *__diarrhea__*, *__abdominal pain__*, *__severe inflammation__* of the *colon (__colitis__)*, *__fever__*, an *__elevated white blood cell count__*, *__vomiting__*, and *__dehydration__*.

I experienced diarrhea induced by antibiotics and bacteria in your stools. I almost died from the side effects of the cancer disease.

♥ **Gi Gi** ♥

Chapter 8

T O THIS DAY, I feel fearful of having two more years to go before the chance to be cleared to have some form of a normal life.

I am reminded of 2 Timothy 1:7 (KJV)⁷ For God hath not given us the spirit of fear, but of power, and of love, and of a sound mind.

God did not give me a spirit of fear. It must have come from the enemy, the devil.

The bible tells us of Satan's plans in John 10:10 (KJV)¹⁰ The thief cometh not, but for to steal, and to kill, and to destroy: I am come that they might have life and that they might have it more abundantly.

These were the days of my life "Through It All" with God watching over me, who guided me through the chemotherapy sessions.

I persevered.

Positive start,
Endure to the end,
Remain in the race,
Stay committed,
Encourage yourself,
Visualize the end,
Exercise determination,
Reach for your goal,
Embrace victory

Look at me! Here I am today, never giving up on the this and that days that I went through.

Therefore, God kept me motivated and alive. I thank God for the wisdom and belief in me during this time.

With all my faith, I was experiencing the test of a lifetime.

Just like the old sayings go, "your test becomes your testimony," and "our messes become our message," and my faith only grew stronger and stronger every day.

I knew then that this was God's way of giving me a sense of direction, part of that direction was to be seen by a good team of oncology doctors. With God's guiding hands, he gave the grace and mercy to see me thru the toughest of times. When I needed the most help, the Lord wrapped me into His healing arms.

My husband, mom, sister, brothers, and dear children kept me from giving up on life. My family continuously reminded me about the future and what I had waiting ahead of me. That future that was ahead of me provided us with a beautiful granddaughter. We were blessed with another grandson two weeks later to our growing family. Six months later, we added another grandson.

These adorable new additions to our family were even more incentive to fight for my life. Now I have three precious grandchildren. The Lord was blessing me with new life springing up all around me!

With all of that, while dealing with the diagnosis of my cancer. I never dreamed that I would have the chance to hold and cuddle them. God gave me a second chance, and I am still walking with faith and believing in his promises. To God be the Glory.

> Romans 4:20 (KJV) 20 He staggered not at the promise of God through unbelief; but was strong in faith, giving glory to God;

At this writing, we have another beautiful granddaughter, also two more handsome grandsons—lastly, the blessing from having another granddaughter being born. Overall, a total of seven grandchildren that God gave me my life back to enjoy.

When I heard them call me Gi Gi, my whole life was worth living. I want to say thank you to everyone who stood by me praying day after day—especially my husband, who is the love of my life. I thank God for my mom, one sister, and three brothers for their love and support. Also, relatives, very dear friends, and co-workers as well. They were also there when I needed them.

There is a saying about how your friends will always be there to lift you off your feet. But it takes a special angel to remind you of how to spread your wings and remember how to fly.

And I had my "Through It All" angels praying for my colon cancer to go away. One day, it was told to me to stop my stinking thinking. Quit your negative ways and be more positive. Remember to praise God's name because, according to the scriptures, the Lord has fearfully and wonderfully made us.

Psalms 139:14 (KJV) ¹⁴ I will praise thee; for I am fearfully and wonderfully made: marvelous are thy works; and that my soul knoweth right well.

❤ You Are What You Eat ❤

Chapter 9

I REALLY CANNOT COUNT all the many blessings that I received "Through It All," and I am still very much surviving, standing with faith.

So, this is my belief. It is never too late to give up on life if you think about it long enough. However, where there is a will to survive, there will be away. We only have one life given to us. Our body is the temple of God. So, we need to treat our bodies well and eat healthy nutritional foods.

The saying goes, "you are what you eat." It is up to you what you put into your stomach to keep on the right path of a good healthy diet.

It does make a significant difference in the end. So, remember to eat plenty of fruits and vegetables, especially tomatoes. Tomatoes control many diseases, and cancer is one of them.

This fruit/vegetable is the epitome of a cancer-fighting superfood. Not only do tomatoes contain lycopene, the antioxidant phytochemical that also helps prevent heart disease, but they are a good source of vitamins A, C, and E -- all enemies of cancer-friendly free radicals.

Tomatoes can prevent many problems for that one person. That is why we should enjoy each day because life is so beautiful and priceless. Just like a butterfly, it appears for a while and then flutters away fast before our eyes.

Sometimes we just lose track of time. It is essential to never take life for granted. Because we are all on borrowed time, so, remember to read your bible because the word is like a two-edged sword. It is a part of the armor of God to get the faith and beliefs of your salvation from God's word.

I truly believe life is a gift from God, but God's gift to us is life and what we make of it is our gift back to God.

As the scriptures mention in James 4:13-15 (NIV), [13] Now listen, you who say, "Today or tomorrow we will go to this or that city, spend a year there, carry on business and make money." [14] Why, you do not even know what will happen tomorrow. What is your life? You are a mist that appears for a little while and then vanishes. [15] Instead, you ought to say, "If it is the Lord's will, we will live and do this or that."

It reads, what is life? It is even a vapor that appears for a little time and then vanishes away. Verse 15 says instead you ought to say; then if it is the Lord's will, we will live and do this or that.

Look at me; it has worked out for me so far! I am living proof. I trusted in the Lord to make me cancer-free. With all my beliefs, I have continued in my faith and God's grace.

The this and that days, where you fight for your life and go through so many struggles. Day after day of receiving chemotherapy and radiation treatments at the same time. While continuously throwing up because of the poison from the chemo.

It makes you so sick, and there is nothing that seems to make you feel better. The sickness must run its course. God's grace and love for me were the medicine that got me through this dreadful ordeal.

The doctors could not prescribe anything to truly take away the horrifying, painful sensation of the pain. I knew I must keep faith that God is in control of my life with colon-rectal cancer.

For an individual, this was hard to grasp. That is why you must have God's grace, which becomes your faith that no one can ever take from you.

♥ God's Grace ♥

Chapter 10

I WISH IT COULD be that simple to tell and show a person what faith is all about. As if you could touch and rub against that one individual human being like a magnet. Well, sorry to say it is not that easy. You must know and believe in God's grace with his control, no matter the situation you are going through.

On good or bad days, he is not visual where you can see him. God is in your heart, which is where you get your faith from knowing God's grace.

Like you have heard about a mustard seed being the grain of faith, it is supposed to be smaller than a grain of salt but produces excellent faith.

Another scripture says in Hebrews 11:3 (KJV) ³ Through faith, we understand that the worlds were framed by the word of God so that things which are seen were not made of things which do appear.

That is why we do not comprehend how God's grace can conquer all. I do believe that God's way and faith were my only way out. By trusting the plans that were being prepared for me to make it through the colon-rectal cancer disease.

I did the next to impossible, that was, for instance, getting up from my bed and keeping motivated enough to go to my job and then having treatments of radiation and chemo. It was only because of my faith to strive and put one foot in front of the other, and I did not think twice about looking back.

I want to tell you that people who believe in themselves, especially with God's pathway, can do anything they put their minds to do. Things are harder and harder to go through without your faith and believing God's plan for us in our world today.

This world is not fair, and nothing makes sense. You cannot trust our president to lead you in the right direction and to keep the USA safe and well. That is why I encourage the next person who has any doubt to read the scriptures in the (KJV) bible and learn about God's ways and plans.

Now, after the cancer effects are over and my body is healing little by little. I feel my life is coming back to me. I am glad that the design of hyperbaric chambers helps to get people healthier. It was my way of having a second chance in life. And to live a happy, regular life as well.

I am thankful for getting to see another birthday and spending days with my family. I am incredibly grateful to have spent a magical night on a Cinderella carriage ride with my wonderful husband. It was for our 21st Valentine's Anniversary! It was a night to remember.

I thank God every day for letting me live "Through It All," standing by faith because you never know when your time is up. Someday we will go home to be in the presence of our Lord, the creator of all things.

It is up to us to get it right in the Lord's eyes and to receive the gift of salvation from this earthly evil way of living.

We should strive to live life's most precious moments to the utmost. The scriptures remind us that the days of our lives have been numbered. No one knows when this world will come to an end. My suggestion to anyone out there that believes Jesus Christ came to be crucified and died on the cross. To save all of us who believe, from our sins. It is better to stay close to the word of God and never let the devil's worldly deeds destroy our faith.

Anything that too good to be true, nine times out of ten times, is a strong possibility of being right. Just remember God is in control of all living creatures, and he is the only one to make all things in our life possible.

So, when the coming of the rapture days begins, the saved ones will go to heaven.

> (KJV) Psalms 96:10-12 [10] The days of our years are threescore years and ten, and if by reason of strength they be fourscore years yet is their strength labor and sorrow; for it is soon cut off, and we fly away.
>
> [11] Who knoweth the power of thine anger? Even according to thy fear, so is thy wrath.
>
> [12] So teach us to number our days, that we may apply our hearts unto wisdom.

The lords return; how long? Well, nobody truly knows except our Heavenly Father.

Before it is too late, remember to let all repent of their sins concerning yourselves. I want you to know this last and final belief of having strength in the Lord is your way into the pearly gates of heaven.

Where you never have pain or sickness, or sorrow. Just remember to ask Jesus to free you from worldly evil sins before it is too late.

We never know when our life will quickly fade away.

♥ The Unknown ♥

Chapter 11

T HESE ARE THE unknown issues that a person struggles with when being diagnosed with cancer. I remember it was like going down a dark, scary road, where you have no idea of what lies ahead. All you know is that you have been diagnosed with cancer while facing the fact that you need Chemotherapy and Radiation treatments. I believe this is another life-threatening condition that the doctors do not fully convey to you.

I will try to explain some issues that most people endure while going through this terrifying rough patch of conditions. I felt that I was not completely informed about the medical, physical, and emotional trauma involved in having cancer. I also thought that the doctors did not adequately prepare me for all the pain and suffering my body would undergo during this experience. For instance, test after test, I am telling you now that these are some of the trials that one must deal with during our condition and treatments.

Chemotherapy is one of the questions to research thoroughly. Find out all you can about the distress it will have on your body and the way that it makes your body feel.

Let me explain what I went through, and many others around me were facing the same difficulties that came with a similar diagnosis. The mental and emotional trauma was bad enough when I started the chemo and radiation treatments. That is when I discovered that I was truly living out a nightmare.

I noticed my teeth were getting brittle and discolored, and I developed lesions on my gums. I also got a thrush mouth, and I had cold chills in the heat of the summer. My skin was dehydrated and scaly, and I bled at the end of my fingertips. I became extremely nauseous to the point where I could not eat or drink anything to save my life.

Prayerfully, one day I just prayed to God to help me make it through this dreadful time. I slowly started eating again and developed a strong will to live. I lost a lot of weight, down from 125 lbs. I lost a significant amount of body mass, and I also agonized over losing my hair.

I just gave up on my nutrition altogether, and to tell you the truth, I was getting to where I did not have any desire to carry on. It was hard for me to focus on what was important in my life, and for me, that was my family, my work, and my friends.

I was trying to hold onto the intense feeling of my faith that sustained me "Through It All." It is essential that you believe and trusts that there is a pathway to Jesus' footsteps. Sometimes a person needs A Hug,

"A Hug!"

It's a wondrous thing a hug can do.
A hug can cheer you when you are blue.
A hug can say, "I love you so,"
Or, "Gee, I hate to see you go."

A hug is "Welcome back again."
And "Great to see you" or "Where have you been?"
A hug can soothe a small child's pain.
Or bring a rainbow after the rain.

The hug! There's just no doubt about it.
We scarcely could survive without it.
A hug delights and warms and charms
It must be why God gave us arms.

Hugs are great for Mothers and Fathers
Sweet for Sisters and swell for Brothers
And chances are your favorite Aunts
Love them more than potted plants.

Kittens crave them, Puppies love them
Heads of State are not above them.
A hug can break the language barrier
And make the dullest day seem merrier.

So stretch those arms without delay and . . .
GIVE SOMEONE A HUG TODAY!
Anonymous

I went through thirty-five treatments of radiation targeting the tattooed area on my body. It feels like a hot blow torch piercing your body for forty-five minutes. The radiation left a red rash and spots on my bottom. It also left an indescribable vibrating pain that stays in your body because of the radiation.

The entire process was constantly wreaking havoc on my body from the inside out. Not to mention the tiresome examinations and testing that you must go through. These are some of the processes the doctors do not thoroughly discuss with you.

These are a few standard procedures and tests that you will undergo during your journey with cancer. They are the CAT scans, PET scans, and MRIs, to name a few. Then you will experience blood transfusions. You will also receive a port that goes into your chest to your heart for easy access to the IVs for injecting medications.

For your information, some of the meds they prescribed with the chemotherapy and radiation can cause bacterial infections.

One example is C Diff, another life-threatening disease that I developed twice, and almost I died from this infection.

It was caused by not getting my immune system built back up from all the infections in my body. There is, however, a medication called anti-biotics that are supposed to cure the conditions. In this case, it did not work very well towards my illness. It worked more against me than it did for me. I was still having diarrhea and bleeding from the rectum. It was a very uncomfortable feeling with the worst pain you could have imagined. The C Diff severely hurts until the medication wholly resolved It.

As time was continually passing by, my body was beginning to shut down day after day. I was still carrying on, and I was even more determined for my life to get better. It was hard to do after the second tragic experience with C Diff. I was undoubtedly getting worried about how to defeat the infections that were running rampantly through my body.

The doctors did not sit down and tell me about the potential aftereffects of the hyperbaric oxygen chambers, in which I had sixty sessions.

Hyperbaric oxygen chambers are tools used for medical treatments. They are supposed to help you regain your energy and help to restore healing to your body. Hyperbaric oxygen therapy has been utilized at times to treat numerous medical conditions, including cancer. Your body's tissues need an adequate supply of oxygen to function. When tissues are injured, they need even more oxygen to survive. Hyperbaric oxygen therapy increases the amount of oxygen your blood can carry. An increase in blood oxygen temporarily restores standard blood gases and tissue function to promote healing and fight infection.

I went to my sessions before my scheduled workday. For most conditions, therapy lasts approximately two hours. A member of your health care team will monitor you and the therapy unit throughout your treatment.

During hyperbaric oxygen therapy, the room's air pressure is about two to three times normal air pressure. The increased air pressure will create a temporary feeling of fullness in your ears — like what you might feel in an airplane or at a high elevation. You can relieve that feeling by yawning or swallowing. Chewing a piece of gum may also help to ease this feeling.

After hyperbaric oxygen therapy, you may feel tired or hungry following your treatment. It does not typically limit any of your everyday activities.

I started treatments before working a full eight-hour day. It was not the easiest thing to do, but I continued this routine at first. The treatments were causing chronic fatigue, and I felt run down. My legs and arms felt like noodles.

I did not quit working, as I sensed God was telling me never to give up. I was trying to stay strong-willed while knowing that God is the one that brings us into a better life. As I was approaching the thirtieth treatment, I would say that the very confined area that they put you into is scary at first, especially if you are claustrophobic. I knew it would make me feel more energized and more alive because I still had my faith in the doctor's care and that the treatments were going to work. I believed it would benefit my body and me as I was going through this journey that I have traveled.

It suddenly appeared that the doctors might have found a treatment to help people become healthier and revived again. There is one more thing to ask your doctor, and that is about going through survival training. Ask questions, like how long it takes to start feeling your old self again after the wear and tear of what cancer does to your body. It is a vicious cycle.

I can tell if you are a strong-willed person who believes and are determined to survive, you can do anything you put your mind to do.

For example, I struggled with 90 sessions of survival training, it was a tough time in my life, but I knew it would be better for my family and me. Especially my husband and kids and grandchildren that were being born during the conditions of my health issues.

I hope people can find true faith in the Lord and believe! The bible tells us what faith is,

> **Hebrews 11:1 (KJV)**
> **11 Now faith is the substance of things hoped for, the evidence of things not seen**.

I have personally seen the power of faith, and it has guided me **"Through It All."**

Five years later and I am living a healthier life with my loving husband.

I am a cancer survivor!

♥ *Dedication* ♥

I dedicate this book to all of those who are
fighting, surviving, and still battling cancer.
There is hope at the end of your journey!
Today is ours; let's live it!

Today

**Today is ours, let's live it
And love is strong, let's give it
A song can help, let's sing it
And peace is dear, let's bring it
The past is gone, don't rue it
Our work is here, let's do it
Our world is wrong, let's right it
Today is ours, let's take it**

Originally written by Beah Richards

♥ About the Author ♥

"THE TROUGH IT All" book was written by Linda Thomas, who happens to be a first-time writer. She has been happily married for 25 years to Jimmy Thomas and still standing in faith together. They have five children and eight grandchildren. She is a woman of faith and has a big heart that holds others' feelings more than herself.

To the people who know her well, they will understand that one should always take care of yourself first. It is essential that you are healthy and happy because you will have faith when you believe in God. When others see your faith in God, there will always be a blessing of happiness for the next individual who survives cancer.

I've been writing about my colon cancer journey for many months now, roundabout three years or more. I had no idea that my colon cancer experience would have turned into a book that originated from the writings in my "Lady of Faith" journal. One day, I decided to turn my writings into this book after sharing my papers with family and friends, that proofread my book's chapters.

It has been my experience to stay persistent in your combination of writings and finding the motivation and the will to live. My faith in God and my desire to fight through this obstacle called colon cancer have allowed me to express my thoughts and feelings to the unknown believers in the world. "God can take the mess of our past and turn it into a message. He takes our trials and tests and turns them into a testimony."

In my opinion, I believe there are goals out there that anyone can attain if you believe in God and have faith. God has blessed me with a beautiful spirit and a heart of gold and to this day,

"I am still surviving"!

Printed in the United States
By Bookmasters